GOLDEN GOAL 1

BOY WONDER 9

A CHAMPION AGAIN 19

ROCKY HOCKEY 29

PETER THE GREAT 37

STATISTICS 44

CONTENTS

With the eyes of the world

watching, Peter came up

big for Sweden in the 1994

Winter Olympics.

CHAPTER ONE

Golden Goal

Sunday, February 27, 1994, was a day Peter Forsberg—and all of Sweden—will never forget. It was the last day of the Winter Olympics at Lillehammer, Norway, and the Canadian and Swedish hockey teams were facing off for the gold medal. Both teams were eager to play. Canada hadn't won hockey gold since 1952. The Swedes had never struck gold in Olympic hockey. Later that day one of these teams would be crowned the new Olympic champion.

After 60 minutes of end-to-end action, the score was 2–2. Peter had assisted both of Sweden's goals. Since there wasn't a winner, the teams played a 10-minute sudden-death overtime period. But even after that, the score was still tied.

The gold medal would be decided by a shootout. Five players from each team would take penalty shots against the other team's goalie. The team with the most shootout goals would win the game. Canada won the coin toss to decide which team would shoot first.

Petr Nedved, playing for Canada, was the first shooter. He whipped a wrist shot over the glove hand of Tommy Salo, the Swedish netminder. Sweden's first shooter, Hakan Loob, was stopped by Corey Hirsch, the Canadian goalie. Next, Paul Kariya made it 2–0, beating Salo high to the glove side. The second Swede, Magnus Svensson, fooled Hirsch to make it 2–1. The next three shooters, two for Canada and one for Sweden, all failed to score.

Peter goes to the net in the 1994 Olympic gold-medal game.

Peter was the fourth shooter for Sweden. The Swedes desperately needed a goal to tie the game. He could feel the pressure of the whole country on his shoulders.

At the center-ice faceoff dot, Peter picked up the puck and skated toward the net. Then he looped to his right, almost touching the faceoff dot outside the blueline. Across the blueline, he glided in on Hirsch, moving to the left and bringing the puck toward the middle of the ice. He cradled the disk on his forehand, as if he were going to shoot. Hirsch

moved out to cover the angles. Suddenly Peter cut back to the right and tucked a backhander between Hirsch's pads and into the net. That tied the shootout score 2–2.

Each team had one last shot for Olympic glory. But Canada's Greg Johnson and Sweden's Roger Hansson both missed chances to be national heroes. After the first shootout round, the game was still tied.

Next came the sudden-death shootout. The teams would take turns shooting until the tie was broken. Because Canada shot first in Round 1, Sweden went first in the second round. Svensson led off. He had beaten Hirsch twice, once in the third period and again in Round 1. He sped in on Hirsch and fired. The goalie made a clutch save. Then Nedved had a chance to win the gold for Canada, his adopted country. He went in and deked Salo. Nedved had a wide-open net, but his backhander dribbled wide.

Next up for Sweden was Peter. As he got ready for his shot, he remembered a magical move that former Swedish star Kent Nilsson had used in the 1989 World Championships. Peter thought it was one of the greatest goals he had ever seen. Three times Peter had tried the same move playing for MoDo in the Swedish Elite League. Three times he had missed. Now, though, Peter would try to repeat Nilsson's magic.

Just as he had on his first penalty shot against Hirsch, Peter looped to the right as he crossed the blueline. He drifted left and moved in on the goalie. Once again, Peter cradled the puck on his forehand. Would he shoot this time? No! He deked to the left. Hirsch went to his knees and slid left. Then, as Peter was still moving to the left, he pushed the puck to the right and almost lost it.

Stamp of Approval

Peter Forsberg's dramatic Olympic gold-medal winning goal was commemorated on a Swedish postage stamp in 1995. Fifteen million copies of the stamp were issued a month before the World Championships, which were played in Sweden that spring. The stamp cost about 50 cents. It could be used to mail a letter anywhere within Sweden, or Sverige, as the Swedes call their country.

But he recovered and, with only his right hand on his stick, barely shoveled a backhander under Hirsch's glove and into the net. It was one of hockey's most spectacular goals. And the timing couldn't have been better.

Instantly the Swedes had a 1–0 lead. But they hadn't won yet. Canada still had one more shot. Kariya, who had scored once in the third period and again in Round 1, had one last chance to tie the game. The 9,245 fans at the rink, including Sweden's King Carl Gustaf, and millions more watching on television around the world, were breathless as Kariya skated toward the Swedish netminder. Salo went down, and Kariya fired the puck high to the glove side. But not high enough. Salo kicked up his left leg and made the save.

Sweden had won Olympic gold! The Swedish fans went crazy. Swedes at home danced in front of their television sets. A mob of Swedish players crushed Peter. He had scored the golden goal, the biggest one in Swedish hockey history. Not bad for a boy from a small northern town.

THE PETER FORSBERG FILE

Position: Center

Born: July 20, 1973, Ornskoldsvik, Sweden

Height: Six feet (1.83 meters)

Weight: 190 pounds (86 kilograms)

Shoots: Left

Number: 21

Nickname: Foppa

Favorite Foods: Pasta, oatmeal

Favorite Actor: Adam Sandler

Off-Season Sports: Golf, tennis

Hobby: Sleeping

Childhood Hockey Hero: Hakan Loob

Hockey Highlights: Stanley Cup victory, Olympic gold medal

In the rinks of northern

Sweden, Peter learned

the skills he would need

to be an NHL superstar.

CHAPTER TWO

Boy Wonder

Peter Forsberg learned to play hockey in Ornskoldsvik (pronounced *Urn-shoulds-veek*), where he was born on July 20, 1973. Ovik—as Swedes sometimes call it—is on the east coast of Sweden, about 225 miles (350 kilometers) below the Arctic Circle. The city of 56,650 people is famous for its pulp and paper company and for the hockey players it sends to the National Hockey League (NHL).

Like most boys in Ovik, Peter caught the hockey bug early. He looked up to his older brother, Roger, who played the game at a local sports club. Since Roger was a hockey player, Peter wanted to be one, too. By the time he was four years old, he had learned to skate. When he was six, he joined the same club as his big brother. Their father, Kent, coached at the club, which was sponsored by MoDo, the local pulp and paper company.

When Peter was a boy in Ovik, NHL games weren't televised there, so unlike boys in Canada and the United States, Peter never pictured himself playing in North America. Instead, he dreamed of playing for MoDo's team in the Swedish Elite League. "I watched every game when I grew up, every single one," he remembers. Peter's dream eventually came true. When he was old enough, he played for MoDo's Elite League team.

Growing up in Ovik at the same time as Peter was Markus Naslund, who now plays for the Vancouver Canucks. Naslund, who is 10 days younger than Peter, played for Jarveds, a different club. Over the years, the two boys played each other often.

Peter led all scorers at the 1993 World Junior Championships.

Naslund recalls the first time the two played against each other: "I think we won 9–8 and we each scored seven goals."

But Peter has different memories of that first game. "You may have scored seven goals, but I didn't," he says modestly to his pal. "You were much better than I was." The boys were the best players on their teams. "It was basically me against Peter," Naslund remembers.

Peter's team may have lost that first game, but its luck changed over the years. "One of the best memories from

my childhood was winning our hometown hockey tournament in 1988," he says. It was the last year the boys would
play against each other in Sweden. The next season
Naslund joined MoDo.

Their boyhood rivalry made Peter fiercely competitive.
"I wouldn't accept losing to his team and he wouldn't accept

losing to my team. It was like war," Peter declares. His foes in the NHL say Peter's will to win makes him a tough opponent to play against.

Peter joined the MoDo Juniors in 1989–90. The next season, when he was only 17 years old, he played for both the MoDo Juniors and MoDo's senior team in the Swedish Elite League. His play with the juniors really caught the attention of professional scouts. He scored an amazing 102 points, including 38 goals, in only 39 games with the junior squad. Many of his 64 assists were setups on goals scored by Naslund, then his linemate.

On June 9, 1991, the NHL held its annual Entry Draft in Buffalo, New York. It was a big day for two young men from Ornskoldsvik. Peter was chosen sixth overall by the Philadelphia Flyers. Ten picks later, the Pittsburgh Penguins selected Naslund.

That September, Peter stayed in Sweden so that he could attend high school. He also had a place on the national junior team. During the regular season, he played for MoDo's Elite League team, which was coached by his father.

Over the Christmas holidays, Peter got his first taste of international competition at the World Junior Championships. Sweden

Hockey Town

The tiny city of Ornskoldsvik sends more than its fair share of players to the NHL. Besides Peter Forsberg, players listing Ovik on their birth certificates include Markus Naslund (Vancouver), Daniel and Henrik Sedin (both Vancouver) and Niklas Sundstrom (San Jose). There are other former MoDo players, such as Anders Eriksson (Chicago) and Mattias Timander (Boston), playing in the NHL, too.

placed second to Russia. Peter finished second in tournament scoring with 11 points in seven games. He had better luck in May when he played for Sweden at the World Championships in Prague, Czechoslovakia. The Swedes defeated their arch-rivals from Finland to win the gold medal.

A year after he was drafted by the Flyers, Peter was traded to the Quebec Nordiques (now the Colorado Avalanche). The Nords had drafted Eric Lindros first overall in 1991, five picks before Peter. But Lindros refused to sign with Quebec, claim-ing the team wasn't serious about winning. So, on June 30, 1992, the Flyers sent Peter, five other players, two first-round draft choices and $15 million to Quebec in return for Lindros.

Peter still wasn't ready to play in the NHL. Instead, he played for MoDo's Elite League team in 1992–93. The World Junior Championships that season were held in Gavle, Sweden, about 225 miles (350 kilometers) south of Ovik. Peter had a tremen-dous tournament. He set a record for points scored (31). His line, with Naslund and Niklas Sundstrom as wingers, set another record for points (69) in just seven games. Both marks still stand. Peter was named best forward and made the all-star team. But for the second year in a row, he and his teammates had to settle for the silver medal. They lost only one game, 5–4, to the Canadians, who got the gold. Peter had one goal and three assists in the loss.

In 1991 Peter was drafted by the Philadelphia Flyers.

When MoDo's season ended, Peter had 47 points, good enough for second place in the Elite League. The players voted

him the league's most valuable player. It was the first time a junior-age player won the MVP honors. "I don't think I really deserved it," he said modestly.

The Nordiques, who had missed the playoffs five of the last six seasons, really wanted Peter to play in the NHL in the 1993–94 season. But Peter had other plans. He wanted to play for Sweden in the 1994 Olympics. He signed a four-year, $6.5-million contract with Quebec in October 1993 that allowed him to play in the Olympics. He agreed to join the Nords when MoDo's season ended.

After his Olympic heroics, Peter returned to MoDo. He finished third in league scoring and was MVP for the second year in a row. Then, in the playoffs, he caught fire, setting a record for postseason scoring and leading eighth-place MoDo to the finals. By the time the Swedish playoffs ended, the Nordiques' season was over. Once again, Quebec had missed the playoffs. Peter and his new NHL teammates would have their work cut out when they reported to training camp in September.

ACADEMY OF HOCKEY

At 16, Peter Forsberg entered the ice hockey academy program at Nolaskolan, a high school in Ornskoldsvik. Students in the three-year program take regular courses such as mathematics, science and languages. They also spend class time studying hockey tactics and practicing the game.

Only 20 of the best 16-year-old players in Sweden are accepted into the program each year. According to Peter Blomqvist, the headmaster (or principal) of Nolaskolan, Peter earned good grades in his regular subjects. Top marks are required of all students in the ice hockey academy program.

Once in the NHL, Peter

quickly established

himself as one of hockey's

top young players.

CHAPTER THREE

A Champion Again

Peter spent the summer work-
ing out and was in top shape
when he arrived at the Quebec Nordiques' training camp in
September 1994. The Nordiques were counting on a big
season. The team had lots of talent. Quebec's lineup included
good young players such as Joe Sakic, Mike Ricci and Valeri
Kamensky. Missing the playoffs the previous spring was a
big disappointment. Over the summer, the Nords appointed
Pierre Lacroix general manager. He wasted no time making
changes. He hired Marc Crawford as the team's coach and

made several trades. "When I was hired, it was to get this team back on track, to make it an instant winner," Lacroix said.

The Nords were counting on Peter, too. His play in Sweden had earned him the title as the "best young player *not* in the NHL." Now that he was in the NHL, he would have to perform.

Peter was one of the top forwards at camp. He impressed everyone with his pinpoint passing. "He must have four eyes," said winger Chris Simon. "Two in front and two in back." He showed that he was tough, too, digging in the corners and knocking people off the puck.

But as Peter looked ahead to his first season in the NHL, he saw a storm cloud. There was a disagreement over money between the owners and players. The owners decided not to hold any games during the dispute. The lockout, as it was called, lasted until January, when the NHL started a shortened, 48-game schedule.

Peter was the first Swede to become NHL Rookie of the Year.

Quebec's first game was a 3–1 win in Philadelphia on January 21. Peter got his first point, an assist on the winning goal, against the Flyers, the team that had drafted and traded him. Six days later, in his third game, Peter scored his first NHL goal in a 7–3 loss to the Buffalo Sabres. After 20 games, though, the Swede had only three goals and 14 points. It was a slower start than he had hoped for. But in the last 28 games, he got hot, notching 12 goals and 24 assists. His late surge earned him the Calder Trophy as NHL Rookie of the Year and a place on the NHL All-Rookie Team.

The Nords had the league's second-best record during the regular season. They were heavily favored going into the playoffs. But Quebec faltered again, bowing out in the first round to the New York Rangers, the defending Stanley Cup champs. It meant an early start to another summer of change.

That change began on June 21 when the NHL approved the sale of the Nordiques to a company in Denver, Colorado. The team would play the next season as the Colorado Avalanche. The Denver fans were happy to have hockey back in town. From 1976 until 1982, the Colorado Rockies had played in the Mile High City before becoming the New Jersey Devils. In their six seasons, the Rockies were terrible, making the playoffs only once. The Avalanche, on the other hand, was one of the best teams in the NHL.

Pierre Lacroix wasn't finished making trades. Before the season started, he traded for Claude Lemieux. The rugged winger was the Devils' most valuable player when they won the Stanley Cup in June. Then, in December, Lacroix pulled the trigger on a trade to get superstar goalie Patrick Roy from the Montreal Canadiens. Roy had led the Canadiens to two Stanley Cups, but he had fallen out of favor with the team's management.

On the ice, the Avalanche showed its new fans it could win at high altitude. In mid-October, the

Same Game, Different Rink

The rinks in Europe are about 13 feet (four meters) wider than the surfaces used in the NHL. The big ice gives an edge to good skaters, who have more room to move. Physical players prefer the smaller rinks, where it is easier to bodycheck. "It's more fun to play on a smaller surface," says Peter Forsberg, a good skater who likes to mix it up.

Avs began an eight-game winning streak. Peter struggled early on. Through eight exhibition and eight regular-season contests, he failed to get a goal. "I had five or six breakaways, missed them all, and I hit a couple of posts," the frustrated Swede said.

But his coach, Marc Crawford, wasn't worried. "He was getting assists, winning faceoffs and getting scoring chances. The puck just didn't go in for him," Crawford said.

Again, however, Peter finished strongly. By season's end, he was fifth in NHL scoring, with 116 points in 82 games. Colorado finished strongly, too, ending up with the second-best regular-season record. Once again, the team was favored to do well in the playoffs. This time it wouldn't disappoint.

The Avs eliminated the Vancouver Canucks—with Peter's old friend Markus Naslund—and the Chicago Blackhawks in the first two series. Then it was on to Detroit. The Red Wings were the best team during the regular season. They had set the league record for most wins (62) in a season. Beating Detroit would be a tough chore for the Avs. Colorado took early control of the series by winning the first two games. The fast start enabled the Avs to upset the Wings in six games. In the last game, Peter scored an awesome goal. Breaking down the left wing, he slipped the disk between the legs of Red Wings defenseman Nicklas Lidstrom,

Best at Both Ends

Peter Forsberg is one of hockey's best two-way players. As proof, look at his 1996–97 season. Despite missing 17 games, he led the Colorado Avalanche in scoring with 86 points. At the other end of the ice, Peter finished second in voting for the Frank J. Selke Trophy, which the NHL awards to the "forward who best excels in the defensive aspects of the game."

MCNEEL MIDDLE SCHOOL
BELOIT, WISCONSIN 53511

who seemed frozen like a statue as Peter skated around him and deposited the puck behind Detroit goalie Chris Osgood. Peter's marker erased any doubt about which team was going to the finals.

Like the Avs, the Florida Panthers had never been to the final series. Playing in only its third season, Florida had never even made the playoffs before. The surprising Panthers had clawed their way to the finals behind the incredible goal-tending of John Vanbiesbrouck. They were underdogs as the series began.

Colorado won the series opener 3–1. Then, in the first period of the second game, Peter took charge, popping three goals and leading the Avs to an 8–1 drubbing of the Florida squad. The Panthers never recovered. The fourth and last game, featuring stellar play by both goalies, was the longest scoreless match in finals history. It lasted 104 minutes and 31 seconds before Uwe Krupp's slap shot beat Vanbiesbrouck. Less than a year after leaving Quebec, Peter and his team-mates were Stanley Cup champions!

SWEDISH HAT TRICK

There are three major championships in hockey: the Stanley Cup, the Olympics and the World Championships. In Sweden each of these titles is represented by a crown on the jersey of the national team, which is nicknamed Tre Kronor, or Three Crowns. Peter Forsberg's dramatic shootout goal to win the 1994 Olympics meant three players—Tomas Jonsson, Mats Naslund and Hakan Loob—became the first Swedes to wear all three crowns. Peter, who won gold at the 1992 World Championships, completed his hat trick when Colorado captured the 1996 Stanley Cup.

One of hockey's best

stickhandlers, Peter

is at his very best

when he has the puck

in heavy traffic.

CHAPTER FOUR

Rocky Hockey

Summer was short for Peter. On June 12, 1996, two days after the Avalanche won the Stanley Cup, Denver held a victory parade for the champions. An estimated 200,000 fans crowded the downtown streets, wildly cheering their heroes. Then, two days before his summer ended, Peter took the Stanley Cup where it had never been before—to Sweden. Peter and Stanley attended a public ceremony hosted by Elvy Soderstrom, the mayor of Ornskoldsvik. Afterward, Peter and his pals had a party at the Forsberg family home.

Between celebrations with the trophy, Peter spent the summer staying in shape. He was a member of Sweden's World Cup team, which began play on August 26. Most major tournaments are played during the NHL season, and many of the best professional players can't take part. But the World Cup was held before the NHL season, so all the top players were available. It was the first time Sweden's finest pros, such as Mats Sundin and Peter, played together on the national team.

Sweden had no problem qualifying for the playoff round. In the semifinals, though, the Swedes ran up against Team Canada. The game was a heartbreaker. The teams battled to a 2–2 tie after 60 minutes. In sudden-death overtime—next goal wins—both teams had plenty of chances to win, but neither had scored as the final minute of the second extra period began to tick away. Then, with 12 seconds left, Theoren Fleury beat Tommy Salo to steal the victory for Canada.

Peter is especially dangerous in close with the puck.

During the 1996–97 regular season, the reigning Stanley Cup champs lived up to their reputation. They finished with a league-leading 107 points. Peter wasn't so lucky. In a game against Calgary on December 14, he was kneed by Flames defenseman Todd Simpson. He suffered a severe charley horse in his left thigh and missed 17 games. While he was recovering, the Avs signed Peter to a two-year contract extension worth $13.6 million.

A Stanley Cup repeat wasn't in the cards for Peter and the Avalanche in 1997. In a rematch of their showdown with

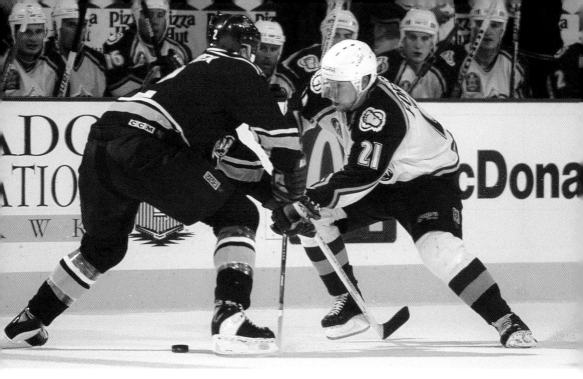

Detroit a year earlier, the two rivals met again in the Western
Conference finals. This time, however, the Red Wings were
the better side. After knocking the Avs out in six games,
the Wings went on to capture the Cup.

Peter was third in NHL scoring when the league took a
two-week break in February for the 1998 Olympic Games in
Nagano, Japan. The break meant NHL pros, including Wayne
Gretzky (Canada), Mike Modano (United States) and Mats
Sundin (Sweden), could make their Olympic debuts. Sweden,
the defending Olympic champion, was a gold-medal favorite.
But the Swedes lost to Finland and Canada in the opening
round and didn't qualify for medal play.

Colorado went into a slump after the Olympics. Nine of the Avs had played in Japan, and Joe Sakic had been injured there. In late March, Peter hurt his groin and missed seven games. The team won just eight of its last 22 games. Despite all of this, Peter potted 91 points, enough for second place in the league scoring derby.

The Avalanche opened the playoffs against Edmonton. Although Peter managed two goals in Game 1, the Oilers won 3–2. Then, in the second game, Peter exploded for two goals and three assists, and Colorado evened the series with a 5–2 win. Inspired by Peter, the Avs stormed to a 3–1 series lead. Peter managed 11 points in the first four games. But he was shut out in the next three games, which the surprising Oilers won, eliminating the Avs.

Colorado's early exit from the NHL postseason left Peter free to play for Sweden at the World Championships in Zurich, Switzerland. After his country's poor showing in the Olympics, Swedish coach Kent Forsberg was under pressure to win. The Swedes were almost perfect, taking the gold medal with a record of nine wins and one tie. The coach's son tallied 11 points in seven games and was named to the all-star team. For Peter, the victory had extra meaning. "It was a very special feeling to win with my dad," he said proudly.

Heads Up

Peter Forsberg is one of hockey's best stickhandlers. "It's amazing the way he handles the puck in traffic," New Jersey Devils goalie Martin Brodeur observes. Keeping one eye on the puck and the other on his opponents is a skill Peter learned as a boy in Ornskoldsvik. "It is hard to teach," his father, Kent Forsberg, says. "But I would always tell him, 'Look up, look up.'"

The Avalanche began the 1998–99 season with four straight losses. The team had a new coach, Bob Hartley, and it took time for the players to learn his system. At the end of December, Colorado had 16 wins, 17 losses and three ties. It was the club's worst record since moving from Quebec. Again, Peter's year started slowly, but he picked up the pace as the season progressed. On March 3, the Avs visited the Florida Panthers. With two minutes left in the second period, the home team led 5–0. Then Peter got serious. He scored once before the end of the second, and added two goals and three assists in the final frame as the Avs roared past the Panthers 7–5. This time Colorado was hot as the playoffs opened.

The Avs met the Red Wings, their old foes, in Round 2 of the postseason. Detroit, attempting a Stanley Cup "three-peat," looked impressive as it won the first two games. But the Avs swept the next four and moved on to Dallas to face the Stars in the Western Conference finals. After five games versus Dallas, Colorado seemed in control with a 3–2 lead. Peter was hurting, though. In Game 4, he had been hit by Stars defenseman Richard Matvichuk and had injured his left shoulder. In the last two games, he was unable to add to his league-leading 24 points, and the Avs lost both contests. The Stars later defeated the Buffalo Sabres to claim the Stanley Cup. Peter spent the summer—and the first two months of the next season—recovering from major surgery to repair his shoulder.

Peter leads his team on a rush out of the Avalanche zone.

Peter's on-ice intensity

is just one reason

he is considered the

best all-round player

in the NHL.

C H A P T E R   F I V E

Peter the Great

The scouting report on Peter reads like an NHL general manager's Christmas wish list. He is an excellent stickhandler and one of the NHL's top passers. His awesome wrist shot makes him a feared sniper. He is a rugged competitor who plays with intensity at both ends of the ice. He is strong on his skates and can perform his skills at top speed. It is the combination of all these talents that makes Peter a superstar. And that's why every team in the league would love to have him.

Many hockey experts say Peter is the best all-round player in the NHL. In April 1997, *The Hockey News* published a survey of NHL coaches and general managers who were asked, "Eric Lindros or Peter Forsberg, who's better?" It was an interesting question because five years earlier Peter was one of six players traded for Lindros. The vote wasn't even close. Eleven of the 15 asked chose the Swede. "Determination, size, strength, speed, skill, pick your poison, because Forsberg has it all," one anonymous insider said. "And you can't overlook the fact that he has already won an Olympic gold medal and a Stanley Cup."

His opponents are equally impressed by the All-Star Swede. "Peter is, as far as I'm concerned, one of the most complete players in the league," Toronto Maple Leafs captain Mats Sundin says. "He's always a threat offensively, but he's really, really strong at both ends of the ice. I think that's Peter's greatest asset—his ability to be a two-way player."

It's not surprising that Sundin, a Swede, places such a high value on defense. "In Sweden we play more defense than they do in North America," says Peter's father, Kent. The elder Forsberg taught the importance of defensive play to Peter when he coached him on MoDo.

Centers of Excellence

A key to the Colorado Avalanche's success is its pair of star centers—Peter Forsberg and team captain Joe Sakic. Opponents hoping to beat the Avs must stop two top lines. First, they have to shut down Sakic's line. Then they have to keep Peter and the second line off the score sheet. "In Joe Sakic and Peter Forsberg, the Avalanche can perform the same kind of magic I saw night after night when I played in Edmonton in the 1980s, with Wayne Gretzky centering one line and Mark Messier the next," former Oilers goalie Grant Fuhr says.

But not every one agrees that good defense is Peter's greatest talent. His first NHL coach, Marc Crawford, thinks Peter's intensity is his chief strength: "Whether it's on offense or defense, when he goes after the puck he gets it. Always. Of all the assets he has in his game, that is clearly his best."

Those who face him on the ice agree. Markus Naslund, his longtime friend, says, "He wants to win at everything he's doing. If you play Ping-Pong or you play video games with him, there's always a big battle. I think that's one thing that makes him a great hockey player—that he hates to lose."

Even Peter knows he's competitive. "If I went out there and wasn't prepared to give it everything I had in order to win, then I'd be in bad shape. You've got to constantly be able to push yourself and do whatever it takes to help your team win. I don't really know any other way of approaching the game."

If Peter has a weakness, it's his habit of passing when he's got a chance to shoot. Like most great playmakers, he almost always has twice as many assists as goals. "Most of the people

TOUGH ENOUGH

When Swedes first began playing in the NHL in the early 1970s, they had reputations as highly skilled players who usually avoided body contact. Former Toronto Maple Leafs owner Harold Ballard once joked about Inge Hammarstrom, one of his players, that "He could go into the corner with a pocketful of eggs and never break one of them." But times have changed. Swedish players such as Peter Forsberg and Mats Sundin are among the league's most physical. "You see some skill players who don't normally get involved physically," Colorado general manager Pierre Lacroix says. "Not Peter—he hits so hard it's unbelievable."

who watch me say I don't shoot enough," he admits. "If I see a player in a better position, I usually pass it. I don't care about goals, as long as it is good for the team."

Pierre Lacroix is someone who would like to see Peter shoot more. The Avs' general manager signed the Swede to a three-year, $30-million contract in April 1999. At the time, Lacroix noted that since moving to Colorado, the Avs' record when Peter scored a goal is an amazing 69 wins, 10 losses and 12 ties.

Colorado's commitment to build a Stanley Cup–winning team is one reason Peter signed again with the Avalanche. With stars such as Joe Sakic and Patrick Roy also penned to long-term deals, Peter has reason to be hopeful. "We're going

to be good in the future, and I want to be part of that," he said. In March 2000, the Avs traded for superstar defenseman Ray Bourque, a move that many hockey insiders felt would clinch the championship for Colorado.

After missing 33 games due to injuries during the 1999–2000 regular season, Peter entered the postseason in top form. But despite his team-leading 15 playoff points, including four game-winning goals, the Avs fell to the Dallas Stars in the dramatic seventh game of the Western Conference finals. For Peter, though, the dream of another Stanley Cup remains as strong as ever.

STATISTICS

National Hockey League (NHL)

Regular Season

Year	Team	GP	G	A	P	PIM
1994–95	Quebec	47	15	35	50	16
1995–96	Colorado	82	30	86	116	47
1996–97	Colorado	65	28	58	86	73
1997–98	Colorado	72	25	66	91	94
1998–99	Colorado	78	30	67	97	108
1999–2000	Colorado	49	14	37	51	52
Totals		393	142	349	491	390

Playoffs

Year	Team	GP	G	A	P	PIM
1995	Quebec	6	2	4	6	4
1996	Colorado	22	10	11	21	18
1997	Colorado	14	5	12	17	10
1998	Colorado	7	6	5	11	12
1999	Colorado	19	8	16	24	31
2000	Colorado	16	7	8	15	12
Totals		84	38	56	94	87

Key

GP = Games Played   G = Goals   A = Assists
P = Points   PIM = Penalties in Minutes

Swedish Leagues

Regular Season

Year	Team	GP	G	A	P	PIM
1989–90	MoDo	1	0	1	1	4
1990–91	MoDo	23	7	10	17	22
1991–92	MoDo	39	9	18	27	78
1992–93	MoDo	39	23	24	47	92
1993–94	MoDo	39	18	26	44	82
1994–95	MoDo	11	5	9	14	20
Totals		152	62	88	150	298

Playoffs

Year	Team	GP	G	A	P	PIM
1993	MoDo	3	4	1	5	0
1994	MoDo	11	9	7	16	14
Totals		14	13	8	21	14

Swedish International Hockey

Year	Event	GP	G	A	P	PIM
1992	World Championships	8	4	2	6	6
1993	World Championships	8	1	1	2	12
1994	Olympics	8	2	6	8	6
1996	World Cup	4	1	4	5	6
1998	Olympics	4	1	4	5	6
1998	World Championships	7	6	5	11	0
Totals		39	15	22	37	36